THE ERROR OF NOSTALGIA

RICHARD BOADA

Texas Review Press

Huntsville, Texas

FIRST EDITION

Requests for permission to acknowledge material from this work should be sent to:

Permissions
Texas Review Press
English Department
Sam Houston State University
Huntsville, TX 77341-2146

Grateful acknowledgment is due the editors of journals in which some of these poems or versions of them first appeared: "Horse Songs" *Rabbit Catastrophe Review*, "Mississippi, Mississippi" *Rabbit Catastrophe Review*, "Walking Backwards to the Tropics" *Country Dog Review*, "Cities of the Dead" *Country Dog Review*, "The Error of Nostalgia" *Sierra Nevada Review*, "Swim Lesson" *Off the Coast*, "Marriage Proposal" *Jabberwock Review*, "Bright Objects By Night" *Jabberwock Review*, "Post-Soviet Recession" *RHINO*, "Louisiana Fugue" *Crab Orchard Review*, "Disaster on Dauphine Street" *Crab Orchard Review*, "Sierra Negra" *Town Creek Poetry*, "Avocado Orchard Fire" *Town Creek Poetry*, "The Bell Ringer of Saint Louis Cathedral" *Bayou Review*, "Record Breaking Heat" *Bayou Review*, "Anatomy of Pluck" *Fifth Wednesday Journal*, "Post-Soviet Nocturne" *Fifth Wednesday Journal*, "Auricular Confession" *Southern California Review*, "Vieux Carré" *Rougarou*, "Modern Glow" *Sakura Review*, "Hemispheric Divide" *Temenos*, "Red Tennessee" *Front Porch*, "Q Street Canal" *The Chaffey Review*, "General Intercession" *Red Rock Review*, "Ecuador's First Olympic Gold Medalist" *Reed Magazine*, "The Ovation" *Yalobusha Review*, "Exposed Veins" *Oak Bend Review*, "Double-Birth" *Birmingham Arts Journal*, "Monotonic Jubilee" *Oyez Review*, "Avocet Coup" *Rio Grande Review*, "Red River Gorge" *Northridge Review*, "Strikes" *Northridge Review*, "Iroquois Manor Shopping Center" *Northridge Review*, "Mercy" *New Madrid*, "Hog Killing Weather" *Touchstone*, "Falls of the Ohio" *Santa Clara Review*, "La Plaza Mayor" *Limestone: A Journal of Art and Literature*, ".25 Cent Cigars" *Poetry East*.

Cover Design: Pier Rodelon
Author Photograph: Victoria Fisher

Library of Congress Cataloging-in-Publication Data

Boada, Richard, 1980-
  [Poems. Selections]
  The error of nostalgia / Richard Boada.
    pages cm
  Poems.
  ISBN 978-1-937875-20-6 (paperback : alk. paper)
  I. Title.
  PS3602.O145E77 2013
  811'.6--dc23
                                            2013013290

For My Family

Contents

I. Archipelago Rising

II. Post-Soviet Recession

III. Horse Songs

IV. Victory Tattoo

THE ERROR OF NOSTALGIA

I. Archipelago Rising

MISSISSIPPI, MISSISSIPPI

The gravity of the tropics retreats
from the hemisphere's ghosts,

toughened mountain chevrons,
condors, and desert of clouds.

I decline the river's invitation to exile
and shrink into mercy.

SIERRA NEGRA

The sun's pink spears
the volcano's skinny
trees. Punishing magma carves

rock, melts palmettos, boils ocean.
Tongues of lava, like pistons,
lap up slope and apron. The caldera

appears wide-mouthed and smoking.
Galapagos hawks fly through ash plumes
toward coastal banks where they will perch

on cacti. The morning sky's fluorescent
hues court grass fires: archipelago sinking.

AVOCADO ORCHARD FIRE

Water-ripe flowers hiss
      and singe upon caloric

contact. The glacial fire
      smothers each fruit, peels

black-green-purple skin,
      smelts pale flesh, does bees'

work, explodes seeds
      for biennial regeneration.

Ash patina veils the trees
      manumitted of form.

CITIES OF THE DEAD

Gall wasps sprout
on spongy wood.

Their tiny carcasses prism
from fires. A thrush swirls

thin limbs, feeds here
in the bog flax and sedges.

Free from the darkness
in the morning spatters,

so many of us resist the torment.
Each lava rock, a votive

prodding the mausoleums
from extinction.

AT DAWN

Pink starfish at low tide
shiver and pulse under bold
constellations that fall in the ocean.
Hundreds escape and bide their shore,
observing dawn, and I move barefoot
among this garden. Flexing limbs,
they stretch ruddy arms and disks
by millimeters, lounge in new mud,
wait for waves. I kneel, trace paths
of mollusks, my fingers in the sand-
tunnels dug by crabs. The waves,
lifting rays of each starfish, cradle
a dead seagull wrapped in kelp.

EXPOSED VEINS

Folding the sun across iced
hollows, aspen shadows engrave

the gorge. Cold descends
and the wind busts once taut

tree bark, limbs and trunks.
Again, birds notch branches

with beaks, they chip away
the frozen primer cleaning out

torpid seeds and leaving only slivers
of walnut and pinecone shell.

Shocked black boughs grope ice spears
that drip in heat, now immobilized.

Night agrees with ice, each fells
the woods and the aspish horizon.

Gummed branches decay with sap
marbleizing in narrow copper trails

that wind over each tree. What's left
of the woods remains for the pecking.

LA PLAZA MAYOR

Her hands are scabbed
and calloused from knitting
thousands of napkins,
place mats, and tablecloths.

Her Quiche accent drowns
in the foot traffic of La Plaza
when she walks away,
calling out what she carries.

I follow, but lose this woman
among the many women
with red-purple,
green and gold cloths
over shoulders, on heads
and around waists.

So many women
calling out what they carry,
like prayers and confessions.

LOS ALBAÑILES

He chops and cubes
pork Fritada. Serves the meat
on corn tortillas. Fries plantains.
Preserved of their sweetness,
they won't taste like meat.

His wife shaves ice with round
metal graters. Pours papaya juice.
Los albañiles form a line
on the street,
buy a plate lunch,
eat the cooked food.

The men chew the Fritada,
slowly, allowing hot
onions and peppers to burn
their tongues just enough.
Each man sits on his cooler.
One speaks of the brief
disappearance of Fidel—nothing new.
Another chain-smokes and tosses
burnt onions.

The wife sweeps around
the old propane stove.
Stray dogs make rounds
for chunks of discarded
pork, rice and peppers. She sweeps
the fallen meat and vegetables
over the curb. The stream of water
heads for the city drain.

STRIKES

I stood in the cab of my mother's pickup pressed
between her back and the vinyl bucket seat. My small

arms clung to her shoulders like a harness, face flushed,
a suitcase on the floor. Her hair smelled of perfume

that stung the throat and I picked at the black mole
on her neck, tugged at the latched silver chain.

Outside the windows, tall volcanoes with permanent
snow. Ash fell from the sky as clouds paced over Quito.

Diesel trucks carried live chickens and hogs. White feathers
flew to our windshield, red hen legs clawed through the wire

cages. I tightened my arms around her as she shifted gears.
Tighter when we crashed through a stack of burning tires.

Tighter as brooms and sticks beat the side doors. I saluted
green and black military police jeeps. Men with helmets

carried guns. Men with handkerchiefs over their faces carried sticks.
People ran in the smoked streets throwing rocks.

MERCY

Aftershocks all day and Guagua Pichincha is on fire. Its mountain steppes singe and burning eucalyptus tastes like cholera. Slick, golden lava tunnels through Quito's houses, invades each laundry room and shower. Basilicas, cemeteries and the airport Mariscal Sucre disappear. The museums that enclose the park and soccer stadium in the slums will not resist. People wait rather than panic. There's nowhere to go. Ash descends invisible at night. There are cries but grandfather is beside me. We smoke cigars and I decide to quit medical school, leave Quito for New York. In America, my best friends could be Irish émigrés that teach me curses in English, to use lunch hour for cards and cabarets. Marry one of their daughters in Brooklyn. Move my family from the borough to the country. My sons teach boys at Sacred Heart curse words in Spanish. Our fathers erase us. Cotopaxi erupts and scorches the valley. Quito's on fire. The cigars almost gone and grandfather in throttled prayer; we're surrounded.

II. Post-Soviet Recession

POST-SOVIET NOCTURNE

I have seen Trotsky in Mexico City
drinking grape Fanta through a wide straw.

He sips the soda from a plastic sandwich bag secured
with thin wire. He holds the bag like a child with hands

cupped waiting for communion. The soda sloshes
in the pouch and in his belly. I have seen Trotsky smuggle

himself into a basilica crowded with tourists. Inside, frescos
on damp walls. He scoots his semi-circular eyeglasses up

and peers deep into the hind legs of the ass that carries Jesus
into Jerusalem. I have seen Trotsky examine the mules on the
    street.

They neigh and huff through wet and cavernous noses, click
on cobblestones with iron shoes. Trotsky's history unfolds

there, in the mules' joints, where he looks for the 21st century,
for Manhattan, for a Sylvia Beach, for a bookstore window to
    climb through.

ECUADOR'S FIRST OLYMPIC GOLD MEDALIST

Jefferson Perez reschedules our interview
over the phone. "We'll meet at *El Crater*
for lunch in three hours." I couldn't

complain, he's walking laps around the soccer
stadium, skimming milliseconds off his world
record. Already at the bar, I scoop un-popped

corn kernels from the fillet of sole ceviche,
flick defective brown pods against the Marlboro
ash tray. I pin my elbows on the glass-top

counter, daily specials hand written in blue
chalk above the refrigerator full of sodas and beer.
My fingers interlock, an awning over a full

Pilsner, pinched limes soak on a square paper
napkin. Perez calls again, delayed, chased
by children, one foot off the ground.

FOR THE STADIUM VENDOR

The stadium vendor stays on her feet the entire match with a steaming hang-neck platform of empanadas de viento. She calls out, "empanadas de viento!" at each concrete step of the Estadio Olimpico de Atahualpa. Atahualpa, the last Inca king. The Inca prefixed the mountain's name with *coto*, Quechua for throat, to mark their ascendancy. Her empanadas de viento, wind not light like namesake, make her shoulders a permanent hunch. Her posture and captive wind; she's a monument.

ÁREA DE SOL

Above the open corridors
they salivate their sons' triumphs.

Men hack up black phlegm and curse the bulls,
Moist fingers rake their afternoon beards.

Flapping programs to cool their faces, neck scarves knotted,
women pray for the picadores on horseback.

The novices thrust banderas on primed skulls.
Bones clack against steel. Shade silvers

and blesses. The bull's oiled ears, bloodless
in the sun, waved to all.

.25-CENT CIGARS

I learned how to roll cigars in Ecuador
from a man who rents a house on an acre of land.
Tobacco stains his face and fingers.
Scars on his forearms and legs –
from a land mine.

In his dry barn, away from the churning
wheels of the plow, he hangs
the wet tobacco, weighs dry leaves,
makes even piles. I pinch loose tobacco
with my fingers on the work table

and watch his wife hang the laundry
on the drying lines
through the open barn door.
Water drips off pants, shirts
and underwear onto the red-brown earth,
like the sweat from his brow. He rolls
leaf after leaf after leaf.

HEMISPHERIC DIVIDE

Vacationing in America, he squeezes bags of brown sugar at the supermarkets. Inadvertently, he breaks through the plastic. Quietly, licks sweet off cuticles. He returns home to La Mitad del Mundo, where monuments mark the provenance of latitude zero. He flashes through shops and pokes each llama wool sweater with straightened index fingers. The fabric sinks, a garbled response to equatorial pressure. He can't resist the sheared masses, spindled and dyed. He places woven finger puppets on each digit to cease the craving, to twitter the carnival of animals—an equine metonymy.

GENERAL INTERCESSION

The bride and groom warned their guests
not to eat the Peruvian squid. Days later,

guests that did not heed caution arrive
at clinics complaining of awkward balance.

Jellied arms appear siphoned of bone.
Thighs, tender and malleable, swallow

kneecaps and collapse into calves. All muscle
floats in skin as each bit of calcium dissolves

into marrow, bone shafts into suckers
and ink valves. From the hips, new arms sprout,

tentacles pucker and squirm. Noses become beaks.
Tiny squids, undigested, brine the intestines,

funnel through arterial orders, coil
in the chambers of guests' hearts.

QUITEÑA

At Peña's finca, the young wife walks over
white stringy vines and dry viscous entrails
of tractor-smashed cassavas. She picks one up

with two hands, like she would a small child.
Her fingers pan over curves and bumps, brush
pine straw and black inch slugs from the oval body.

She checks for mold and rot, carries hers
through the muddy patch, boot heels unplugging roots
from the ground, looking for another.

MONOTONIC JUBILEE

A tape measure clicks out each
centimeter from the mechanical
spool. Her thumb presses the first unit
below her armpit. With dancer's
flexibility, she wraps the tape around
her back to pinch the circumference
of numbers in place. She reads digits
upside down. Her husband's breakfast
on the balcony: milk in coffee cools
to flesh, a finch pecks at the toast. Below,
the Vieux Carré. He's at their hosiery
updating the bookkeeping and lace
inventory: a caliper's bulbous tallies.

VIEUX CARRÉ

Vulcanologists speak of decay,
loss and relic as Pompeii resigns

to malarial grievance, to the alluvial
flats of its harbor. Pompeii's a parapet

fastening the dead to annulment. Their open
mouths sprout fruit and ilex flashes

through vellum bodies. There's a cast
over the immobile leavening.

The sun kilns the Mediterranean,
flecking translucent greens upon

membranous gray. Pompeii's fevering
from tides and thumping magma

underground. An asylum of heat
will rise, the drupe of a womb.

THE BELL RINGER OF ST. LOUIS CATHEDRAL

Her body recoils
like a pistol,

spine whips
and sluices

with each clap
on metal,

with each boom
off dome.

The menagerie
of tongues

and crowns
jettisons tolls.

Hammers smack
bronze curves

and skirts. Each
bell fatigues, cannon

after cannon. She
clasps to ropes,

bells on pulleys
and flat peals

over the square.
She mouths

a dull, bowing,
beautiful.

AURICULAR CONFESSION

She lives simultaneously
in centuries. It's something
remarkable, like a sneeze,

breathless. On accepted Holy Days,
with liturgical veil, she abstains
from sex and breakfast.

But today she will not go
to vespers, will not receive
benediction, will not vow.

On the Metro, her rosary droops
through her knuckles.
The cross, a pendulum bob,

measures the long leaching crawl,
the train's acceleration,
her pilgrimage.

AVOCET COUP

Refugees, second wives, and cowled
monks squeeze through blear
tourists. A corpse floats

on the surface of the Seine. Water chops
and gulps, pounds the scorched
breasts and face. Birds swarm

over. Fledged men on bridges try to snag
the body out of the water with hooking
ash-poles and nets. Timbery sirens call

all to notice. Police arrive with shotguns.
They fire at the chalky sky; abate
the birds from devouring.

POST-SOVIET RECESSION

Without asking, I've been brought a drink
that tastes like melon. Caribbean fruit survives

in La Habana Vieja, dispersed in thimblefuls by waiters.
I often dream of America: trains cutlass prairies,

white smoke blossoms against the postulate of clouds.
Around the corner of the café, a radio plays choppy

méringue and dishwashers jaw about their love affairs,
nicotine stains on their lips. A man off the street stops

at my table, swipes the wedge of lime from the rim
of my water glass. *Limon libre*, he says, looking back.

III. Horse Songs

CANNON BONES

Gray Mississippi spring, unusually cool, spins each tree. Pollen curls from the wide-trunk oaks. Their yellow seeds fury along the muscular canopy of big-leaves, a matrix of flapping and levering. At once, I remember acorns pummeling the tool shed's tin roof. Each metallic spank croaking like the full-throated and spectacularly hungry frog. In this pasture I fasten the colt's saddle for my young daughter who would rather ride on the blanket than the brittle leather. Without knowing, she trusts her ligaments and the colt's to keep them locked and polled. I'm the hare running too fast, crisscrossing an avenue clogged with car traffic. But they're the gift, singular anatomies, cannon bones and fetlocks, phalanxes and skulls, orbiting this coliseum like champions.

RED RIVER

You know how this ends.
The second engine fails.

A Franciscan monk at the window seat
in front of you brokers the young

flight attendant's final confession.
She's been unfaithful to her husband.

Third engine fails. The flight attendant
buries her face in the monk's black habit.

You're aware of absolution. The plane free-falls
and you flip open the cell phone. Don't speed-dial—

press each number. Say goodbye to your girlfriend:
your envoy. She will miss you. Still dry palms

and you regret throwing away the apple
at security checkpoint. You'll never have

its flesh crackle in your mouth, its resurrecting
aroma, pulp cowling your molars. Go ahead

and smoke, take that final isotopic drag.
Look out the window—the river splits

the city, nourishes all those trees.
November's a long abscission.

LOUISIANA FUGUE

The barber has been bankrupt
since the flood. The town's bald,

men and women, no longer visit
since the lakes rose and stunned.

Combs prostrate in disinfecting jars,
once mitochondrial in his hands.

Dozens of tonics on shelves
multiply in lipid mirrors,

refracting electric lights.
The jilted shaving brush and razors

foul rust. The barber can only trim
his bougainvillea's viscous petals.

There has never been winter,
and now red January sludge

anoints, lathers and steams.
Lathers and steams.

DOUBLE-BIRTH

Improbably, two foals clumsily approach
their mare. Thin phalanxes and coffin bones
buckle as hoofs slip in the morning grass.
They trust hock joints, pick up gallop,
one snout knocks the other. Breaths fog
the air. The mare's a quay in bluegrass
panicles and her young are muscular
vessels that fleck moisture off their black
pelage. They'll run this birth coat off.

HORSE SONGS

I'd like to be
your dreamer
going past
razor white
mountains to
Mississippi.
The horses sing
to an open winter.
Their red blood
fizzes, a supernova,
and knows
Yazoo River.
The horse sings,
neighs gray
vapors, and I'm
never too far
from you
never too far
from coming
toward you.

FALLS OF THE OHIO

A tugboat pulls a barge hauling
coal and timber. High mud
water splits. The river's locks
empty and fill, glints
in the current. Downstream,
the falls of the Ohio expose the patch
reef of clams and sponges, golden
rods and stinging nettles wilt. My arm
shudders and I inhale the humid air, suffering
from the altitude of this bridge;
flipped a coin into the Ohio
where Cassius Clay threw his medal.

THE OVATION

This morning I swept the abbey grounds,
raised hours, looked for Thomas Merton's

grave. Like the Trappist, my prayer was labor.
Giant, dry poplar leaves under my feet

lauded, their song sent off rhizomed earth
up limestone sepulchers. In the gift shop,

Abbot Bernard gave me a hunk of bourbon fudge
and directions to the headstone. I never found

Merton, but dulled letters announced others, priests
and sisters long part of Kentucky. Still, I wanted vigil

for Father Louis, as he was known here. Where to leave
the soil from Prades, carried so long in this breast pocket?

HOG KILLING WEATHER

Sows hooked on the walls of the barn,
hind shanks hung raw, bellies split open,
hearts on sawdust, fetlocks swept up in piles.
We saved their hooves in tin pails, chopped
above the phalanx. Mother jarred
and labeled each season.

Slicing bacon, cleaving hunks of pork
for the grinder, I counted scars on my hands.
Palms up, sawed nicks and bites, scabbed
thumbs, pruned as if long soaked in water.
Those blood stained blades and lips of hooks
clipped hands, again and again, buried me inside
the slaughter, fried on the skillets.

RED RIVER GORGE

Teenage boys with buck
knives chip initials
into land bridge
sandstone. Panicked bigleaf
magnolias and yellow buckeyes spit
seeds against the lichen
covered rock arch. Kentucky
augite gouged. The boys call
bird dogs back
to the hollow. Mouths
full of quail, muddied
feathers stuck to snouts
and ears. Shotgun shells
in the nettles. The boys walk
chucking acorns into Red River.
Pouches stuffed
with northern bobwhites.
The covey roosted
near the ground.

Q STREET CANAL

The cashier is no longer afraid of dying.
Tonight, she'll hand customers out-of-ink pens to sign

credit card slips, fidget in the drawer, break
dollar bills and count change incorrectly. After second-shift,

she'll hang her apron in her locker, punch her time-card
right on the hour and slip a dry ballpoint into the front

shirt pocket of the night manager. She'll smile at him,
hop over the customer service counter, snag a pint

of Buffalo Trace whisky and sprint out of the store.
She'll chase the Union Pacific on foot along Kincaid

until it steers away for Bend and Mount Jefferson.
She'll find a grassy quay on the Q Street Canal.

The damp night will soak through her clothes. Fingers of light
from distant cars will dazzle her until she finishes the bottle.

DISASTER ON DAUPHINE STREET

The apartment's living room floor above
the Metro Café collapses. Furniture funnels
down. The sofa, a deadhead freighter,
crashes into the aquarium. Busboys and dishwashers

round up missing crustaceans. Shoeboxes full of letters,
matchbooks and complimentary bars of soap scatter.
The maitre d' and Fire Marshall rule out termites.
From the vestibule a materfamilias stares
at the ceiling's cavity, wires dangling from pink insulation,
elliptical tenets, and her canceled reservation.

ANATOMY OF PLUCK

The Mississippi slouches through Baton Rouge,
present of the present, flattening Louisiana.

There's a tin roof home on the canal to Whisky Bay
under the locomotive overpass where red steam
engines haul freight. A woman in a man's white shirt

that's sweated to the skin sits on knees like a hare.
She unplugs strawberries from their crowns,
looks down a channel of crape myrtles

fossilized in sun. Their pink has become
her moral imperative, her rot.

IROQUOIS MANOR SHOPPING CENTER

The strip mall injects cracking
purple light into low clouds,
infusing free radicals and spreading
laconic weight. Clouds are now
summering and thick, ceiling,
forcing contact, like Biloxi's dusk
heavy upon the gulf. These night
clouds descend on the parking lot,
cars kept running, scrums of shoppers
rolling bascarts with rusty wheels—
unhinged windmills pirouetting
over asphalt. Catfish and fried
noodles from Vietnam Kitchen
upend streetlights, pedestrians
and Peppermint Bar patrons.
The drunk, waiting for taxis, vomit
on the curb. There's no moon,
no Beaux-Art façade, only neon
remains night's docent.

MODERN GLOW

Mississippi 49 resurfaces from clogging
winter snow. Spring's gloom thickens
longleaf pines and inflames the absorbing asphalt.

Night cranes on the hollows and bogs,
pries highway cracks by millimeters.
Unispiraled wire, sheathed in plastic,

compressed beneath the gravel, now sprouts
like switch grass through the unfrozen
road's fault-lines. The ungrounded electric circuits
charge topsoil and flax. Distant light, utterly spent.

MISSISSIPPI WINTER

She wants to be a character in a Jack Kerouac novel,
a Japhy Ryder with hands deep in plush vest pockets,

Lucky Strikes squarely tucked away, black sunglasses,
hair uncombed. She mimics Kerouac's longing
for a destination when she exhales a long gray rope of smoke.

In the still quite morning by the small pond near
her parents' home, beyond the metallic forest, alluvial
earth and sputtering Mississippi sleet, trees riot

in the breeze and slim steel clouds suture the sky. She orbits
the pond like a rickety satellite that's too close to the atmosphere,
iced grass crunching as she walks, and loses a layer of clothes

each circumference. She burns as she closes in
on what's left of her own debris.

MARRIAGE PROPOSAL

Our confession, New Orleans, Conti Street,
feet skating on hosed-down sidewalks,
as if they were iced in the plumb twilight.

The plasmic sun dilutes the faces
of morning pedestrians. They waddle in twos
and threes and fours, like mallards on green,

marshy lawns. We're the gold ponies of a carousel, though,
foals repeating a bobbing gait, affixed to perimeter,
charioting the spherical distance; toneless gallops

in bronze lamé. The men round Pirate Alley, St. Peter's
and Bourbon Street, and we align our insecurities with theirs.
Theirs, the fleeting politics of risk, the returns of sons to mothers,

the opining men of women, theirs are the embalming memories,
the rosy lucidities that appear when one goes home. As much as our
engagement to marry is our own bas relief, a confession raised

hard in stone, our bodies, consecrated in the waters of this town,
become evidence of who we are, and where we will never be.

IV. Victory Tattoo

CORPS DE BALLET

In unison, they unlock elbows and fan birdwings, each pink breast emboldens. I see this in dusky silhouettes and shadows against a bamboo window shade. I'm in the backyard with my wife fixing supper on the grill; the girls in the corps de ballet are our neighbors. I rotate corn on the cob in its husk. Its water drips on charcoal, and flames pirouette up through the grate like the prima ballerina. I've taken no short cuts with this meal, long roast for the Cornish hens in garlic and parsley baste, braised portabellas and spinach soufflé. The corps de ballet continues to rehearse in the living room of their duplex. Pointes on dry hardwood floor, toes crinkling in slippers. I tell my wife that we're more complex than a bayou, and our meal fills. But this night is strange and elegant, and this somewhere is a place still with heart trouble and invisible wrens next door.

RANKS OF HOUSES

We submit personal facts
for the total record.
There's a man's voice on the radio,

yelping, and the neighbors
make love all morning. Transfixed
on the moaning, springs unlatching

from the box-spring, mugs in the cupboard
streak, and the neighbors come,
hands pressing firmly on the drywall,

irremovable prints on once
polar-white paint, She'll index
all moments like this. Dark

trees in the yard, enameled in ice,
bowing wide. Our vicious
tones, our marriages, and what we let

go, miles of sluicing sleet;
a total monotony. She knots
her expectations of

our lives' summaries
into an autopsy that reveals
unnatural causes of death.

SPEED OF EVENTS

She plays
Townes Van Zandt
on the juke
to teach me
a lesson
in physiology.
She racks
the cold-smooth
billiard balls, spins
chalk on the rail
and preens wrist
muscles. Her
greening eyes
remind me of
an old lover
from Louisville.
If she leaves me,
I wouldn't take it
too bad, but what
is it that keeps
us together?

RECORD BREAKING HEAT

The new cat sharpens his claws
on furniture like a welterweight,

flares of druidic enterprise conducted
in pawing jabs. He sheds everywhere

and gnaws at the hibiscus brought in
from freeze that never came,

its flowers stunned and recessed.
My toddler in the other room must

resent me and the plastic mattress cover
that sticks to his naked limbs and back.

In bed most of the time, I sweat through
sheets, but there's a new binary—

the cat instead of my wife sleeps on my chest
and he sharpens his claws,

leaves lobes of blood where
he walks and kneads at night.

COLOPHON

We spend my birthday in Oxford, Mississippi
and rent a room in the guesthouse of a young couple.
They promise a big breakfast of eggs, hash browns,
biscuits and coffee. My wife falls backwards onto
the king-sized bed, stretches her arms and legs like
a snow angel. I pull off her western boots. The cat
that slinked around the courtyard between the guesthouse
and the main house now pushes its face against the netting
of the porch door. The air smells of cheese, barbeque and pine.
In the evening, we walk to the old town square and find a bookstore
where a writer reads from a new novel. One character in the book
knows someone that has been shot in the head. During the Q&A,
the author confirms that he knew a drug dealer who had in fact
been shot during a deal gone wrong. Back in the guesthouse,
after making love, my wife confesses the very same to me.
This fall night, full of noise, animals cooing for mates,
I forget that she is a widow, that I am a second-husband
and that we are just at the beginning.

BRIGHT OBJECTS BY NIGHT

There needs to be a table in his empty kitchen,
a stolid mahogany, color of cigar, a place to wait for spring.

The kitchen window, the threshold of his language, the portal
likely to shift thought to verbalization, remains shut.

This is the enchantment, the sublimation of bird chatter into wind,
a chalky half-life of Mississippi woodpeckers and longleaf pines,

cicadas dazzling underground, a wasp that has trapped a honeybee
in the womb of a rose, a raceme of white flowers that sprouts along

the hedge of the neighbor's garden. The young wife in hospital
    scrubs
tracks footprints through the house and into the empty kitchen.

When she is gone, he'll dream of medical waste: infected needles
and bruise colored bandages covered with spores and fungus.

But for now, they'll march together through the apartment, and
    she'll sop
the evidence of her labor with a wet towel.

SWIM LESSON

He swallows his buoyancy, cheeks inflate, lungs fill
with the gross gulps of pool-water. The bloom

of his airy voice fizzes upward in a globe. His language
drags in the deep. He resists expelling his breath and flits

his legs toward the surface. His body's a dizzy flare,
a palimpsest and nostalgic. His body's a morning in Paris,

garbage trucks rumbling on the brick roads, barges weighing
down the Quai de la Seine, glints off a stained glass window

trailing the sun slats on the river-water. In the pool, their bodies
are now the magnificent branches of city trees reaching across a
    boulevard,

interlocking limbs and flowering big leaves. All ripples disappear
when he stops galloping in the water and leans into her body,

his skinny forearms grazing her muscles. Her hands firm
on his pelvis, his body drowsy. She turns him on his back

to transform him into a streaking comet. He pliés
against the translucent water and relies on her brightening hands.

MISSISSIPPI SOUND

The shower of their first-floor duplex sputters
cold and salty. Biloxi's winter now scallops
the young wife's body, and she asks her husband
to fix the temperature. She's been in the gulf and needs
to wash off the silty morning, needs heat to latch.
Sunrise the color of pumpkins; a colic, a basin,
an imposition between them. She swims
each morning, far and far and far. But she returns to shower.
She cannot go beyond the waist-deep water, the semaphores,
the permanent distance.

WALKING BACKWARDS TO THE TROPICS

He lies facedown on a white mattress,
a helix of stitching, jacquard and paisley,

with arms crisscrossed at the wrists. His neck
is as tight as a military officer's in a pressed

and buttoned shirt. In the dream he does not write
to her. There's petroleum on his tongue possessing

his language. He negotiates terms,
conditions for surrender, and some things

important to them before. But the colors in
his mind are lava, mint, and cadaver-skin

gray waiting for autopsy. In the dream
he refuses her, but she's a freighter

on an Andean highway twisting and
self-propelling toward the tropics.

She's a poet's lyric stirring backwards
from the precipice, a crushed letter within

an envelope, a galaxy, a Bachata, and their bodies
were once continents scrambling against torsion.

THE ERROR OF NOSTALGIA

The city clangs
in the rain
and smog.
Each city-tree
tastes of violence;
bird chatter
harpoons the wind,
tapers in alleys.
There's a young
couple making love
in a sedan.
There're January
tornados and grade
school safety drills.
Students muddle,
form lines and file
through hallways
full with tan steel
two-story
lockers. The real
fury is standing
paired and pressed—
a gut full of joy.

VICTORY TATTOO

Morning workouts at Churchill Downs, and the colts edit the track hoofing and plunging their pin-like legs into the slop. Few spectators in the grandstand, fewer in the paddock, hold off wavy April rains. Tornado sirens beating across the county echoing in church bells before the morning call to post. This organism challenges us to bet against it; supple neighs from clear-pink lungs, fecund-brown coat, trim silks and bridle. A storm gathers speed in the Ohio valley; it once caramelized dews over Texas hill country. I'm chanting at them all like the monk's vesper, "go on, go on, run, run." Jocks' goggles choked in slop. Jocks' thick slop breaths. Whips flick draughts of wind-choked mud. Silks earth-greased and racing form numbers indistinguishable. I haven't a prayer bold enough to get through.

About the Author

Richard Boada is the author of the chapbook *Archipelago Sinking* (Finishing Line Press), nominated for the 2012 Mississippi Institute of Arts and Letters Poetry Award. He is a graduate of the Center for Writers at the University of Southern Mississippi, and won the Sara-Jean McDowell Award at the University of Louisville. Recent work appears in *RHINO*, *Crab Orchard Review*, *Yalobusha Review*, *Jabberwock Review*, and *The Louisville Review* among others. He teaches creative writing at Millsaps College.